REGIONS OF THE UNITED STATES
EXPLORE THE SOUTHWEST

by Kristine Spanier, MLIS

pogo

Ideas for Parents and Teachers

Pogo Books let children practice reading informational text while introducing them to nonfiction features such as headings, labels, sidebars, maps, and diagrams, as well as a table of contents, glossary, and index.

Carefully leveled text with a strong photo match offers early fluent readers the support they need to succeed.

Before Reading

• "Walk" through the book and point out the various nonfiction features. Ask the student what purpose each feature serves.

• Look at the glossary together. Read and discuss the words.

Read the Book

• Have the child read the book independently.

• Invite him or her to list questions that arise from reading.

After Reading

• Discuss the child's questions. Talk about how he or she might find answers to those questions.

• Prompt the child to think more. Ask: New Mexico is part of the Southwest Region. How do you think this state got its name?

Pogo Books are published by Jump!
5357 Penn Avenue South
Minneapolis, MN 55419
www.jumplibrary.com

Library of Congress Cataloging-in-Publication Data

Names: Spanier, Kristine, author.
Title: Explore the Southwest / by Kristine Spanier, MLIS.
Description: Minneapolis, MN: Jump!, Inc., [2023]
Series: Regions of the United States
Includes index. | Audience: Ages 7-10
Identifiers: LCCN 2021057313 (print)
LCCN 2021057314 (ebook)
ISBN 9781636907260 (hardcover)
ISBN 9781636907277 (paperback)
ISBN 9781636907284 (ebook)
Subjects: LCSH: Southwest, New—Juvenile literature.
Southwest, New—Description and travel.
CYAC: Southwest, New.
Classification: LCC F785.7 .S67 2023 (print)
LCC F785.7 (ebook) | DDC 979--dc23
LC record available at https://lccn.loc.gov/2021057313
LC ebook record available at https://lccn.loc.gov/2021057314

Editor: Jenna Gleisner
Designer: Molly Ballanger

Photo Credits: Martin M303/Shutterstock, cover (left); miroslav_1/iStock, cover (right); Felix Mizioznikov/Shutterstock, cover (bottom); Ryan DeBerardinis/Shutterstock, 1; Bob Pool/Shutterstock, 3; YinYang/iStock, 4; Glasshouse Images/Alamy, 5; North Wind Picture Archives/Alamy, 6-7 (foreground); DenisTangneyJr/iStock, 6-7 (background); Ztiger/Dreamstime, 8; PhotoSparks/iStock, 9; Nate Loper/Shutterstock, 10-11; Wingman Photography/Shutterstock, 12-13tl; William Wise/Dreamstime, 12-13tr; Dennis W Donohue/Shutterstock, 12-13bl; IrinaK/Shutterstock, 12-13br; Xarifx/Dreamstime, 14; Kobby Dagan/Shutterstock, 15; Gimas/Shutterstock, 16-17; Zeljko Radojko/Shutterstock, 18-19; THEPALMER/iStock, 20-21l; Thomas Barwick/Getty, 20-21tr; Sean Pavone/Shutterstock, 22t; Doug Meek/Shutterstock, 22m; Badger13/Shutterstock, 22b; Kokoulina/Shutterstock, 23.

Printed in the United States of America at Corporate Graphics in North Mankato, Minnesota.

Title Page Image: Painted Desert, Arizona

TABLE OF CONTENTS

CHAPTER 1
History and Location 4

CHAPTER 2
Geography and Wildlife 8

CHAPTER 3
Daily Life 14

QUICK FACTS & TOOLS
Quick Facts 22
Glossary 23
Index 24
To Learn More 24

CHAPTER 1

HISTORY AND LOCATION

Indigenous people have lived in the Southwest **Region** of the United States for thousands of years. Some lived in Chaco Canyon from 850 to 1250. **Ruins** are still here.

Chaco Canyon, New Mexico

In the early 1800s, **settlers** began moving southwest. The Mexican **government** controlled the land. The United States gained Texas after the Mexican-American War (1846–1848).

In 1854, the United States bought more land from Mexico. This was called the Gadsden Purchase. The land became part of Arizona and New Mexico.

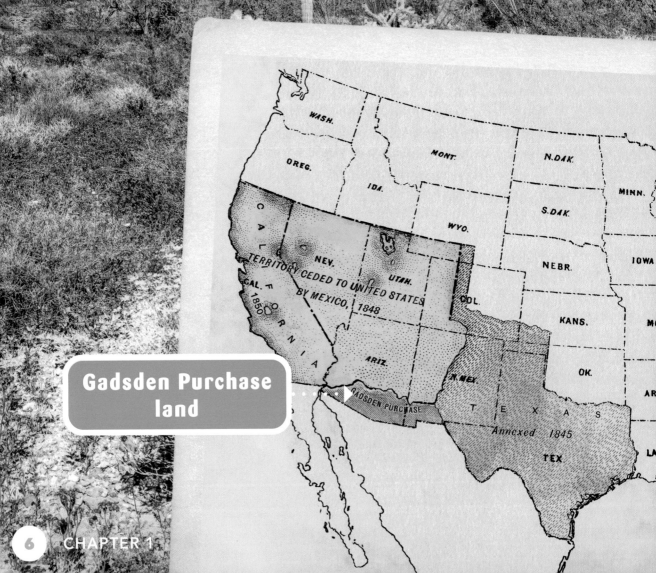

Gadsden Purchase land

TAKE A LOOK!

Which states are part of the Southwest? Take a look!

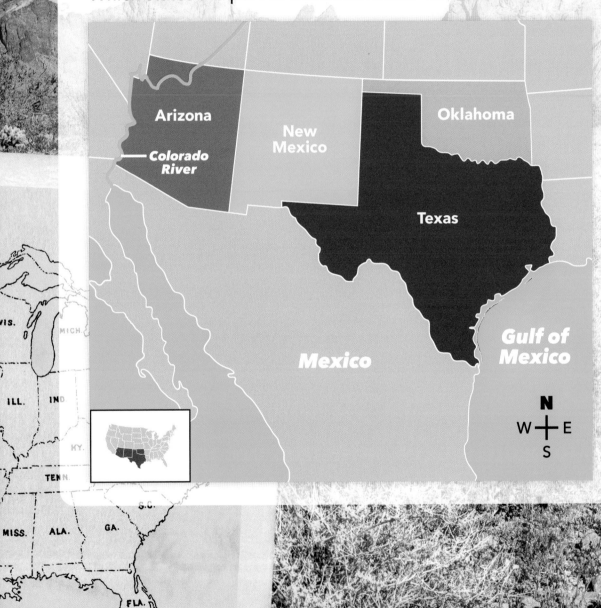

Arizona

Colorado River

New Mexico

Oklahoma

Texas

Mexico

Gulf of Mexico

N
W E
S

WIS.

MICH.

ILL.

IND.

KY.

TENN.

S.C.

MISS.

ALA.

GA.

FLA.

CHAPTER 2

GEOGRAPHY AND WILDLIFE

Many different **landforms** are in the Southwest. **Barrier islands** are along much of Texas's coast. Padre Island is one. It is the world's longest barrier island. Birds, fish, and other wildlife live here.

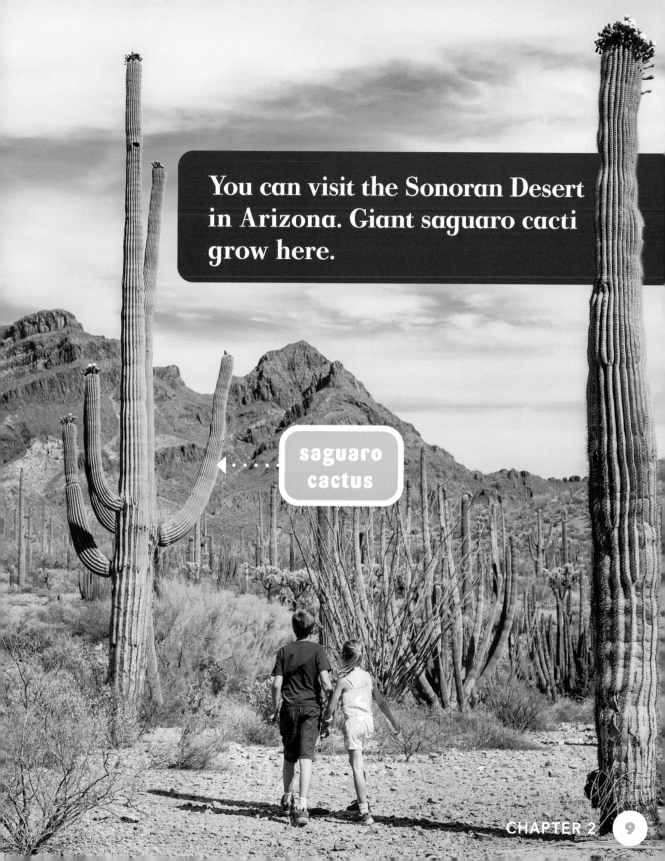

You can visit the Sonoran Desert in Arizona. Giant saguaro cacti grow here.

saguaro cactus

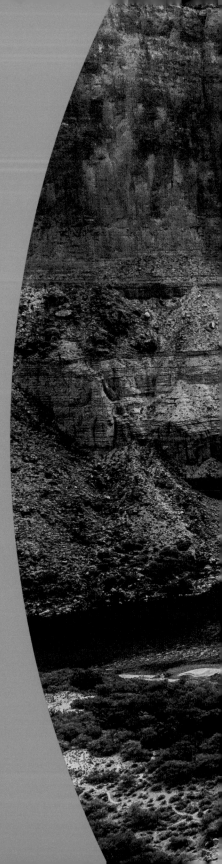

The Grand Canyon is also in Arizona. The Colorado River began carving it more than 5 million years ago. The canyon is one mile (1.6 kilometers) deep in some places.

DID YOU KNOW?

Some rock in the Grand Canyon is more than 2.5 billion years old!

Colorado
River

prairie dogs

armadillo

roadrunner

scorpion

The region's desert is home to many animals. Prairie dogs live underground. This keeps them cool in the hot **climate**. Armadillos have armor. Roadrunners run up to 15 miles (24 km) per hour. Look out for scorpions! They sting!

WHAT DO YOU THINK?

Armadillos have plates that act as armor. They protect armadillos from **predators**. How do you think plates help?

CHAPTER 3

DAILY LIFE

Austin, Texas, is known for live music. You can hear music almost every day here!

outdoor concert

The sky fills with hot air balloons every year in Albuquerque, New Mexico. The Balloon Fiesta lasts nine days. People from around the world come to fly their balloons.

Taos Pueblo,
New Mexico

Some Indigenous people live on **reservations** in this region. Others live on or near **pueblos**.

The homes in New Mexico's Taos Pueblo are made of adobe. This is earth mixed with water and straw. People have lived here for more than 1,000 years!

Many people in the Southwest **mine** for coal and copper. The oil **industry** is also important. Farmers raise **livestock**. They also grow **crops**.

oil pump

TAKE A LOOK!

What are some of the Southwest's top industries? Take a look!

Arizona

New Mexico

Oklahoma

Texas

 = farming   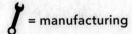 = manufacturing   = maritime transport   = mining

 = oil and natural gas production    = tourism   = wood products

The climate in the Southwest is warm and dry. There is a lot to do outdoors. People hike and ride horses. Do you like to snowboard? You can head to the mountains in winter!

The Southwest is a beautiful part of the country. Would you like to explore it?

WHAT DO YOU THINK?

The Southwest gets very little rain. People **conserve** water. Why do you think this is important? How can you help?

Arizona

New Mexico

SOUTHWEST REGION

Location: southwestern United States

Population (2021 estimate): 42,906,773

Most Populated City in Each State:
Phoenix, AZ
Albuquerque, NM
Oklahoma City, OK
Houston, TX

Top Industries: farming, oil and gas production, maritime transportation, mining, tourism

Average High Temperature:
90 degrees Fahrenheit (32 degrees Celsius)

Average Low Temperature:
40 degrees Fahrenheit (4 degrees Celsius)

Major Landforms: Davis Mountains, Guadalupe Mountains, Grand Canyon, Ouachita Mountains, Painted Desert, Rocky Mountains, Sandia Mountains, Sangre de Cristo Mountains, Sonoran Desert, White Mountains, Padre Island

Highest Point: Wheeler Peak, NM, 13,161 feet (4,011 m)

Major Waterways: Arkansas River, Colorado River, Gila River, Gulf of Mexico, Pecos River, Red River, Rio Grande

Major Landmarks: The Alamo, Carlsbad Caverns, Chaco Canyon, Chickasaw National Recreation Area

OKLAHOMA CITY, OK

CARLSBAD CAVERNS, NM

GILA RIVER, AZ

GLOSSARY

barrier islands: Long, broad, sandy islands that protect the shore from the effects of the ocean.

climate: The weather typical of a certain place over a long period of time.

conserve: To save something from waste.

crops: Plants grown for food.

government: The system by which a country, state, or organization is governed.

Indigenous: Of or relating to the earliest known people to live in a place.

industry: Business or trade.

landforms: Natural features of land surfaces.

livestock: Animals that are kept or raised on a farm or ranch.

mine: To dig up minerals that are in the ground.

predators: Animals that hunt other animals for food.

pueblos: Villages consisting of adobe buildings built next to and on top of one another, built by Indigenous tribes.

region: A general area or a specific district or territory.

reservations: Areas of land set aside by the government for a special purpose.

ruins: The remains of something that has collapsed or been destroyed.

settlers: People who make a home or live in a new place.

The Alamo, Texas

INDEX

Albuquerque, New Mexico 15

animals 8, 13

Arizona 6, 7, 9, 10, 19

Austin, Texas 14

Balloon Fiesta 15

Chaco Canyon 4

climate 13, 20

Colorado River 7, 10

Gadsden Purchase 6

Grand Canyon 10

Indigenous people 4, 17

industries 18, 19

Mexican-American War 5

Mexico 5, 6, 7

New Mexico 6, 7, 15, 17, 19

Oklahoma 7, 19

Padre Island 8

pueblos 17

rain 20

reservations 17

settlers 5

Sonoran Desert 9

Taos Pueblo 17

Texas 5, 7, 8, 14, 19

TO LEARN MORE

Finding more information is as easy as 1, 2, 3.

❶ Go to www.factsurfer.com

❷ Enter "exploretheSouthwest" into the search box.

❸ Choose your book to see a list of websites.

FACT SURFER